3rd Edition

Elementary

MARKET LEADER

Business English Test File

Lewis Lansford

FT Publishing

FINANCIAL TIMES

Pearson Education Limited
Edinburgh Gate
Harlow
Essex CM20 2JE
England
and Associated Companies throughout the world.

www.market-leader.net

First published 2004
Ninth Impression 2018

ISBN 978-1-4082-1972-0

Set in Metaplus 9.5/12.5pt

Printed in Great Britain by Ashford Colour Press Ltd.
Project managed by Chris Hartley

Acknowledgements

We are grateful to the following for permission to reproduce copyright material:

Text

Extract on page 18 adapted from 'Postcard from ... Davos: The hotel with
no staff', *The Financial Times*, 20 April 2012 (Greenwood, S.), copyright
© Susan Greenwood

The Financial Times

Extract on page 13 adapted from 'Billion dollar brains', *The Financial Times*,
23 September 2011 (Dembosky, A.), copyright © The Financial Times Ltd.;
Extract on page 30 adapted from 'The netiquette of working life', *The Financial
Times*, 6 February 2012 (Palmer, M.), copyright © The Financial Times Ltd.

In some instances we have been unable to trace the owners of copyright material
and we would appreciate any information that would enable us to do so.

Contents

The recordings for the listening sections of these tests are on a separate *Test Master* CD-ROM, which is free with the *Market Leader Third Edition Elementary Teacher's Resource Book*. They are also on the *Market Leader* website at *www.market-leader.net*.

Entry test

🔊 **1 Listen to five short conversations. After each conversation, choose the best word or phrase – a, b or c – to complete the sentences.**

Conversation 1

0   The two men are probably .*at work*. .

   a) at home   **b)** at work   **c)** in a taxi

1   The two men talk about ....

   a) a date   **b)** a time   **c)** an address

2   They will have ....

   a) a meal   **b)** a tour   **c)** a kind of meeting

Conversation 2

3   The man and woman are probably in ....

   a) a restaurant   **b)** a business meeting   **c)** a taxi

4   They .... some things.

   a) complain about   **b)** ask for   **c)** ask for information about

Conversation 3

5   The man wants to find ....

   a) a hotel   **b)** the post office   **c)** the train station

6   The man is ....

   a) very early   **b)** very late   **c)** on time

Conversation 4

7   The two men are in ....

   a) a hotel   **b)** a car-hire office   **c)** a restaurant

8   There is a small problem with ....

   a) the price   **b)** the reservation   **c)** the dates

Conversation 5

9   The man wants to buy ....

   a) a ticket   **b)** a snack   **c)** a newspaper

10   The price is ....

   a) €2.50   **b)** two for fifty cents   **c)** 50¢

VOCABULARY

A Match the words with the pictures.

0	a date	i	**15**	a meal	
11	a bill		**16**	a chart	
12	a menu		**17**	an advertisement	
13	a ticket		**18**	a calendar	
14	a price		**19**	a list	

a)
```
SOUP      €12
STEAK     €28
DESSERT   €9

TOTAL     €49
```

b)
BARCELONA
➤ MADRID
Code: B-M001289575-4/11/12

c)
	JANUARY					
M	T	W	T	F	S	S
	1	2	3	4	5	6
7	8	9	10	11	12	13
14	15	16	17	18	19	20
21	22	23	24	25	26	27
28	29	30	31			

d)
SALE NOW ON!
PRICES CUT!✂

e)
To do:
~~schedule meeting~~
~~plan conference~~
call Liam

f)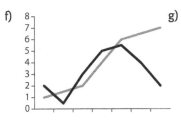

g)

h)
MAIN COURSES
€25
Chicken with pasta
★★★
Roast beef
★★★
Salmon steak

i)
25 MAY
– THURSDAY –

j)
€50

B Circle the odd words out.

0	pizza	pasta	salad	(weather)
20	yesterday	today	month	tomorrow
21	company	manager	worker	owner
22	buy	sell	hire	busy
23	raining	expensive	cold	windy
24	taxi	bus	train	car park
25	India	Japanese	Germany	Poland
26	meeting	computer	photocopier	calculator
27	coffee	tea	cake	water
28	good	fantastic	wonderful	terrible
29	office	hotel room	telephone	meeting room
30	July	Monday	August	December

LANGUAGE   **A**   **Complete the e-mails with words from the box.**

him   his   ~~I~~   it   me   my   you   your

From:	Pierre
To:	Barbara
Subject:	Geraldo Lopez's e-mail address

Hi Barbara!
...... I ......[0] need to contact Geraldo Lopez. Can ....[31] give ....[32]
his e-mail address? Do you have ....[33] in ....[34] phone or
laptop? ....[35] phone is in my coat pocket, at home!
Pierre

From:	Barbara
To:	Pierre
Subject:	RE: Geraldo Lopez's e-mail address

Hi Pierre!
Sorry, I don't have ....[36] e-mail address but you can phone ....[37]
on his mobile. The number is 09932 330 901.
Barbara

B   **Choose the best words to complete the text.**

My company (aren't / isn't)[0] very big. It (has / have)[38] around 40 employees. They
(is / are)[39] from about 15 different countries so the office (is / are)[40] very international.
I (am / are)[41] from Spain and my boss (comes / come)[42] from Sweden. In the office, we
all speak English. We (aren't / don't)[43] usually (have / has)[44] any serious communication
problems.

C Choose the best option – a, b or c – to complete the questions.

0 (A) ...*What*... time is it? B It's eight o'clock.

    a) What b) Why c) How

45 A .... is your first name? B Roald.

    a) What b) Why c) How

46 A .... is the meeting? B At four o'clock.

    a) Who b) Where c) When

47 A .... is your office? B It's in the town centre.

    a) How b) Where c) What

48 A .... are you at home? B I'm ill.

    a) How b) Why c) What

49 A .... are you? B Fine, thanks.

    a) How b) Who c) What

50 A .... is your boss? B Nestor Piccolo.

    a) What b) When c) Who

SKILLS

A Match the sentences with the responses.

0	What's his name?	a)	Yes? How can I help you?
51	How much does it cost?	b)	It's at four o'clock.
52	Where are you from?	c)	It costs €40.
53	What's today's date?	d)	Yes, he is.
54	Excuse me.	e)	OK. That's €20.
55	I'd like two tickets, please.	f)	I'm a salesperson.
56	What time is the meeting?	g)	No, I don't.
57	Steve, let me introduce Adam Jones.	h)	Pleased to meet you.
58	Do you know Ella Myers?	i)	It's the 4th of March.
59	What do you do?	j)	New York.
60	Is Rupert your boss?	k)	It's Octavio.

B **Complete the conversations with the phrases (a–f).**

a)   How about you

b)   How are you

c)   Pleased to meet you

d)   My name's

e)   Where are you from

f)   ~~Hello, Arturo~~

Conversation 1

Tanya   .Hello, Arturo. 0.

Arturo   Hi, Tanya. .... 61?

Tanya   Very well, thanks. .... 62?

Arturo   I'm fine, thanks.

Conversation 2

Simone   .... 63 Simone Dupont.

Ahmed   .... 64, Simone. My name's Ahmed Al-Harbi.

Simone   .... 65, Ahmed?

Ahmed   I'm from Dubai.

READING   **A** **Read the e-mail and decide if the statements are true or false.**

0   The e-mail is to Ilse.   *True*

66   The e-mail is about a computer order.

67   The delivery date for the order is 2nd September.

68   Dimitri asks Ilse for information about the order.

69   Ilse's phone number is 03778 399001.

70   The e-mail is from Dimitri.

Date:	2nd September

Dear Ilse,

Thank you for your order for twenty-two iTab tablet computers. Delivery is scheduled for 16th September.

Your order reference number is 43001.

If you have any questions, please telephone me on 03778 399001.

Many thanks,

Dimitri

B **Look at the telephone message. Choose the best words to complete the sentences.**

0   There ((is)/ isn't) a problem with the order.

71   The message gives (Ilse's / Dimitri's) telephone number.

72   The iTabs are (late / broken).

73   Ilse wants (an e-mail / a phone call) from Dimitri.

74   Ilse wants the iTabs (tomorrow / next week).

75   Helena and (Dimitri / Ilse) work in the same office.

Telephone message
For: Dimitri Barkov
From: Ilse Hopf
23rd September, 10 a.m.
Re: order number 43001
Where are the twenty-two iTabs?
It's very important to have them tomorrow!
Please telephone 04489 733833 as soon as possible!
Message taken by: Helena

C **Look at the e-mail and message again. Complete the sentences with numbers from the box.**

~~2~~   7   10   22   23   24

0   The date on the e-mail is ....2..........nd September.

76   The order is for .... iTabs.

77   The time on the phone message is .... o'clock.

78   The date on the phone message is ....rd September.

79   Ilse needs the computers on ....th September.

80   The delivery is .... days late.-

Progress test 1 (Units 1–3)

A

🔊 2 **Listen to the telephone call. Choose the best word or phrase – a, b or c – to complete the sentences.**

0   Alan works in ...*Technical support*.. .

    a) Marketing   (b)) Technical support   c) Phone sales

1   Sofia has a problem with her ....

    a) telephone   b) computer   c) mobile phone

2   Alan asks about the computer's ....

    a) Internet connection   b) model number   c) delivery date

3   Sofia spells her ....

    a) department name   b) first name   c) last name

4   Alan ....

    a) can send a technician   b) can come to Sofia's office   c) can't help Sofia

5   Sofia has a meeting ....

    a) in the morning   b) in the afternoon   c) tomorrow

B   🔊 3 **Listen again. Complete the form.**

Technical Support Service Request	
Name of caller	*Sofia* ....[6]
Department	...................[7]
Phone number	...................[8]
Office number	...................[9]
Technician appointment time	...................[10]

A **Complete the conversation with words from the box.**

a restaurant   August   Friday   Barcelona   ~~Germany~~   golf   Poland   Polish

A   Is Kasia from ...*Germany*..[0]?

B   No, she isn't. She's from Warsaw, in ....[11].

A   Really? And is her husband also ....[12]?

B   Yes, he is.

A   Does Kasia work at home one day every week?

B   Yes, that's right. She works at home every ....[13].

A   When does she usually go on holiday?

B   She goes on holiday every ....[14]. It isn't a busy month in the office.

    She usually goes back to Poland but last year she went to ....[15], in Spain.

A   Do you and Kasia sometimes play ....[16] at the weekend?

B   No, Kasia doesn't play but we sometimes go to ....[17] after work.

B Match the sentence beginnings with the endings.

0   I don't like going ————

18 Jorge quite likes

19 Pete and Gregor often play

20 Nick works

21 We never listen

22 Susan loves going

23 I usually go on

24 Piet often works flexible

a) to music.

b) holiday in August.

c) watching football on TV.

d) to the gym.

e) hours.

f) out to restaurants.

g) from home once a month.

h) football on Sunday.

C Choose the best words to complete the sentences.

0   I can't move this chair. It's too (light / (heavy)).

25 We can't meet in my office. It isn't (big / small) enough.

26 Liam's presentations are too (long / short). Yesterday, he talked for four hours!

27 My holiday was nice but it wasn't (stressful / relaxing) enough. We were very busy every day.

28 I can't hear you. The restaurant is too (quiet / noisy).

29 I don't like this book. It isn't (interesting / boring) enough.

30 I didn't buy the new Mercedes because it was too (cheap / expensive). I don't have €100,000!

LANGUAGE

A Complete the conversation with words from the box.

are	does	don't	how	is	~~'m~~	what	what's	where	works

A   I 'm.............^{0} Ursula Becker.

B   Nice to meet you, Ursula. My name's David Lopez.

A   ....^{31} you a sales manager?

B   No, I'm not. I work in television.

A   ....^{32} your job?

B   I'm Director of Advertising.

A   ....^{33} do you work?

B   At Channel 10.

A   ....^{34} your wife in television, too?

B   No, she isn't. She works for a magazine.

A   ....^{35} does she do?

B   She's a graphic designer.

A   ....^{36} she travel in her job?

B   No, but she sometimes ....^{37} at the weekend.

A   ....^{38} often does she do that?

B   Two or three times a month.

A   What about you? Do you work at the weekend?

B   No, I ....^{39}.

B **Put the words in the correct order to make sentences.**

0 time What you do work start ?

.......*What time do you start work?*..............

40 afternoon They're the usually in busy .

....

41 the you Why money need do ?

....

42 nine o'clock He's before never work at .

....

43 this much How cost does ?

....

44 sometimes work to walks Dean .

....

45 on work you often How do Sunday ?

....

A **Match the questions with the replies**

0 Where are you from?

46 What's the reason for your visit?

47 Where are you staying?

48 What's your hotel like?

49 How's your business doing?

50 What do you do in your free time?

51 Do you meet your colleagues after work?

52 How many hours a week do you work?

53 What do you like best about your job?

a) I'm staying at the Hilton in the town centre.

b) I'm here to visit my company's head office.

c) I play golf.

d) I work flexible hours, which is great.

e) Between 40 and 50 hours.

f) We're doing quite well.

g) The room is very comfortable.

h) From time to time.

i) I'm from Italy.

B **Match the sentence beginnings with the endings.**

0 Call me back

54 Can I speak to

55 I have a

56 The invoice is

57 There's

58 We can give you

59 Hello, this is

60 I'm very sorry

a) incorrect.

b) a refund.

c) Georg Sipos, please?

d) to hear that.

e) Pat Carter speaking.

f) a piece missing.

g) later, please.

h) problem with my new laptop.

READING **A** **Read the article and decide if the statements are true or false.**

0   Clara Shih is a student.   *False*

61   Clara Shih studied a book called *The Facebook Era*.

62   She worked at Google.

63   Her company is called Hearsay Social.

64   She started her company in Hong Kong.

65   She says starting an Internet business isn't too expensive.

Young CEO

Clara Shih has computer science degrees from Stanford and Oxford, worked at Microsoft, Google and Salesforce and wrote *The Facebook Era*, the first book about Facebook marketing. And all before she turned 29.

In February 2011, she launched her own company. Hearsay Social helps large companies manage their activity on Facebook, Twitter and LinkedIn.

Shih moved from Hong Kong to the US with her parents when she was four. Her parents worked hard and they taught Shih to work hard.

Shih believes that technology allows young businesspeople to make a start because it doesn't cost a lot of money to create a business on the Internet. Now, young people with good ideas have great business opportunities.

B **Read the article again. Choose the best option – a, b or c – to complete the sentences.**

0   At university, Clara studied *computer science*.

    (a) computer science   b) Chinese   c) business

66   Clara Shih wrote about ....

    a) accounting   b) design   c) marketing

67   Hearsay Social .... social networking sites.

    a) sells products through

    b) helps businesses use

    c) introduces people on

68   Shih's parents are from ....

    a) the US   b) Hong Kong   c) the UK

69   The article says Shih learned .... from her parents.

    a) about hard work

    b) Chinese

    c) to use computers

70   Shih says .... helps young businesspeople.

    a) travel   b) education   c) technology

WRITING **Write about your usual weekend. Say what you like to do and what you don't like to do. Write 50–60 words.**

At the weekend, I usually get up at...

Progress test 2 (Units 4–6)

🔊 4 **Listen to the telephone conversation. Choose the best word or phrase – a, b or c – to complete the sentences.**

0 The woman who first answers the phone is probably *a receptionist* .

   (a) a receptionist

   b) a waiter

   c) a company CEO

1 The man .... yesterday.

   a) left a message for the woman

   b) spoke to the woman

   c) placed an order

2 Now the man has ....

   a) some questions

   b) some information for Andrea

   c) a problem

3 The woman says the product has a .... guarantee.

   a) six-month   b) one-year   c) two-year

4 For large orders, the deposit is ....

   a) 100 per cent   b) 15 per cent   c) 50 per cent

5 A large order is more than .... units.

   a) 1,000   b) 100   c) 50

6 For small orders, customers pay ....

   a) 100 per cent when they place the order

   b) 100 per cent when they receive the goods

   c) 50 per cent when they place the order

7 The company has .... units in stock.

   a) 110   b) 100   c) 50

8 The man will probably order .... units.

   a) 110   b) 100   c) 50

9 The man ....

   a) will phone later

   b) places the order

   c) cancels the order

10 The woman offers the man ....

   a) her business address

   b) her mobile phone number

   c) an order number

VOCABULARY   **A**   Complete the text with words and phrases from the box.

| book | ~~buy~~ | check in | collect | go through | take | watch |

I travel abroad for work about once a month. I always ...._buy_......⁰ my ticket and

....................¹¹ my hotel room on the Internet. I carry a small suitcase and I always use an

electronic ticket. So, when I arrive at the airport, I can immediately....................¹² security.

I never....................¹³ the in-flight movie. On the plane, I like to work on my computer.

When I arrive at my destination, I don't have to ....¹⁴ my luggage because

I carry it on the plane with me. I usually....................¹⁵ a taxi to my hotel. After I

....................¹⁶ at the hotel, I usually go for a walk. After a long flight, I need the exercise!

B   Choose the best word to complete the sentences.

0   The waiter usually brings you the (menu / bill) at the start of the meal.

17   Apple pie is usually served as a (starter / dessert).

18   (Cabbage / Salmon) is a type of vegetable.

19   In most countries, you leave a (soup / tip) for the waiter in a restaurant.

20   (Sushi / Tiramisu) is a common main course in Japan.

21   'Bill' in London restaurants means the same as ('check' / 'receipt') in New York restaurants.

22   (Ice cream / Pâté) isn't usually served as a dessert.

C   Make phrases by matching a word or phrase from box A with one from box B. Then use them to complete the sentences.

Box A	Box B
three-year	~~deal~~
free	discount
interest-free	service
a big	guarantee
a low	delivery
after-sales	deposit
~~great~~	credit

0   Yuri got a ..._great deal_.. on his new laptop. The price was low and he also got a printer and a lot of software with it.

23   When I borrowed money for my new motorcycle, I got one year's ....

24   Benny's new smartphone has a .... If it stops working in the next 36 months, the maker will repair or replace it.

25   With expensive products like computers, good .... is important. Customers often have small problems that they need help with.

26   The salesman gave me .... off the price of my new phone – 50 per cent!

27   .... is important for large products like refrigerators because you can't take them home in your car.

28   I ordered my new car from the manufacturer. I paid .... It was only five per cent of the car's price.

LANGUAGE

A **Complete the sentences with the correct form of *do*.**

0   ....Do.......... you have training every April?

29 He .... have a laptop. He says it isn't necessary.

30 .... she have a meeting today?

31 Where .... you usually have lunch?

32 A   Do you know Raymond Smith?

     B   No, I ....

33 They .... come to work on Mondays. It's their day off.

34 A   Do you have any questions?

     B   Yes, we ....

B **Complete the short conversations with *any*, *some*, *much* or *many*.**

0   A   Are there ....any....... cars in the car park?

     B   Yes, there are.

35 A   How .... coffee do we have?

     B   We don't have any.

36 A   How .... days off do you get every year?

     B   21.

37 A   I've just made a pot of tea. Would you like .... more?

     B   Yes, please.

38 A   Are there a lot of engineers in your office?

     B   No, there aren't .... We're all businesspeople.

39 A   Do you have .... soup today?

     B   Yes, we do. We have vegetable soup.

40 A   How .... time do you have free this afternoon?

     B   Sorry, I don't have any. I'm really busy.

C **Complete the text with the correct form (present simple or past simple) of the verbs in brackets.**

My company ....provides...0 (provide) training every year for all employees. Last month, I ....41 (go) on a three-day training course about project management. It ....42 (be) an interesting three days. We ....43 (read) case studies about successful and unsuccessful projects and then ....44 (discuss) them. The quality of the training ....45 (be) always very high and every course ....46 (give) us a lot of useful information.

SKILLS **A** **Match the questions with the responses.**

0	Hello, Hotel Carmen. How can I help you?	a)	Sure. It's a Visa. The number is …
47	How much is the room per night?	b)	I'm sorry, there isn't but you can leave your car on the street in front of the hotel.
48	Can I have your credit card details?	c)	It's €100.
49	Is there a restaurant in the hotel?	d)	Yes, you can. We take all major credit cards.
50	What time do you expect to arrive?		
51	Is there a car park?	e)	Yes, that's right.
52	So that's a single room for two nights?	f)	After 10 p.m.
		g)	I'd like to book a room, please.
53	Can I pay with American Express?	h)	Yes, there is. And it's open 24 hours a day.

B **Complete the conversation at a trade fair with the correct form of the verbs from the box.**

be   close   come   cost   deliver   ~~have~~   include   weigh

A   Tell me about your new MP3 player.

B   What would you like to know?

A   Tell me about the design.

B   Well, it ....*has*........^{0} a unique design. It's the only player on the market now with this type of lid.

A   What's special about it?

B   You can ....^{54} it easily. It protects the player. It makes it very tough. The target market for this model is teenagers who want to look cool.

A   What about colours?

B   Well, it ....^{55} in three colours: red, black or green.

A   It's very lightweight and compact.

B   Yes, it ....^{56} about 150 grams and it ....^{57} just 10 centimetres long.

A   What about the price?

B   If you order from our website, it ....^{58} eighty dollars. The price ....^{59} postage and packaging and we can ....^{60} in three days.

READING **A** **Read the article on page 18 and decide if these statements are true or false.**

0   Fiftyone is a hotel.   *True*

61   Tino Morosani works for a budget airline.

62   Fiftyone doesn't have a reception desk.

63   A concierge helps you with your luggage at Fiftyone.

64   The hotel doesn't offer any kind of food.

65   There are staff at Fiftyone but you don't usually see them.

B **Read the article again. Then choose the best option – a, b or c – to complete the sentences.**

0   According to the article, Tino Morosani ......*owns*...... Fiftyone.

   a)   often stays at

   b)   is worried about the success of

   c)   owns

66   Tino Morosani took the idea for .... from budget airlines.

   a)   reservations   **b)**   check-in   **c)**   advertising

67   In the past, the Fiftyone building had .... in it.

   a)   a car park   **b)**   a reception desk   **c)**   apartments

68   You can book a room at Fiftyone ....

   a)   on the Internet   **b)**   by writing a letter   **c)**   by visiting the hotel

69   You get your key ....

   a)   by mail   **b)**   when you arrive   **c)**   from the cleaning staff

70   Bathrooms are ....

   a)   included in every room

   b)   shared with other guests

   c)   small but beautiful

The hotel with no staff

Fiftyone is a luxury hotel in Davos, Switzerland, but owner Tino Morosani says the idea came from budget airlines.

Morosani wanted to change some old apartments into hotel rooms but there was no space for a reception area or a dining room. Then he thought: Budget airlines have automated check-in so a hotel can have automated check-in, too.

Fiftyone is Davos's first 'automatic' hotel. The entrance looks a bit like a multi-storey car park. There are no staff to greet you. You can't book a room using the phone or e-mail. You must book online. Guests check in with a computer outside the front door. When you arrive, you put a confirmation number into the computer and receive an electronic key, which opens the front door.

The hotel has 24 comfortable rooms and each room has a large bathroom, a balcony and free wi-fi. You can buy breakfast from machines: coffee, apples, bread, orange juice, cereal bars and so on.

You can't see the staff at Fiftyone but they are there. They clean the rooms every day and you can phone them if you have a problem.

WRITING   **Write an e-mail to the Royal Hotel asking to book a room. Use the information in the hotel booking form below. Ask the hotel to confirm the price of the room. Write 50–60 words.**

Booking information:		
Number of rooms:	1	*What is the price for bed and breakfast?*
Type of room:	single, non-smoking	
Number of nights:	2	*Do they have a car park?*
From:	4 April	
To:	6 April	

Progress test 3 (Units 7–9)

LISTENING **A** 🔊 5 **Marco, Susan and Elaine are having a meeting. They need to decide who will lead the South China sales team: Cindy Lee, Tony Wong or Agnes Goh. Listen and choose the best answer – a, b or c – to the questions.**

0   What does Marco say about Cindy, Tony and Agnes?

   a) They work in the Hong Kong office.

   b) They need to choose a team leader.

   c) They speak Chinese.

1   What does Marco do at the start of the meeting?

   a) Gives his decision

   b) Asks Susan for her opinion

   c) Gives his opinion

2   Susan says she prefers Cindy Lee. After that, what does Elaine say?

   a) She thinks Susan is too ambitious.

   b) She asks for Marco's opinion.

   c) She doesn't agree with Susan.

3   At the end, what does Marco suggest?

   a) That they talk to the team

   b) That they chose Agnes Goh

   c) That they decide the next day

B 🔊 6 **Listen again. Match the descriptions with a person. Put a tick (✓) in the correct column.**

		Cindy Lee	Tony Wong	Agnes Goh
0	reliable	✓		
4	hard-working			
5	ambitious			
6	doesn't listen			
7	creative and sociable			
8	too relaxed			
9	practical			
10	not motivating			

VOCABULARY **A** **Complete the sentences with words from the box.**

export   home   luxury   ~~mass~~   niche

0 Nike sports clothing sells to a ......*mass*....... market.

11 High-quality, expensive goods sell in a .... market.

12 .... markets are usually small but profitable.

13 Products sold inside the producer's country are sold to the .... market.

14 .... markets are outside the producer's country.

B **Write the numbers in words.**

0 540 ......*five hundred and forty*......................................

15 6,370 ....

16 29,606 ....

17 902,000 ....

18 4,225,094 ....

19 12.6% ....

C **Match the words and phrases on the left with a word or phrase on the right with the same meaning.**

0 begin —————— a) manufacture

20 make b) sell abroad

21 have a workforce of c) launch

22 export d) employ

23 introduce e) provide

24 supply f) start

LANGUAGE **A** **Put the words in the correct order to make sentences.**

0 were When Germany in they ?
......*When were they in Germany?*......................................

25 company leave the John Did ?
....

26 Lorraine Why Singapore did to move ?
....

27 wasn't work Ivan at happy .
....

28 you have work Do lot a of ?
....

29 Alfredo stressed was Why ?
....

30 a They lot time have of don't .
....

B Look at the three cars. Complete the sentences comparing the cars.

Price	0 Ramon's car is *more expensive* than Anya's car.
	00 Ella's car is ...*cheaper*... than Anya's car.
Speed	31 Ramon's car is .... than Anya's car.
	32 .... car is Anya's.
Fuel efficiency	33 Anya's car is .... than Ramon's car.
	34 Ella's car is .... than Anya's car.
Quality	35 Anya's car is .... than Ella's car.
	36 Ramon's car is ....

C Complete the sentences with the correct form (present simple or present continuous) of the verb in brackets.

0 Every time I go to Singapore, I ....*stay*....... (stay) at the Oriental Hotel.

37 I usually drive to work but today I .... (walk).

38 Martina often .... (call) China. We have three suppliers there.

39 Usually I .... (not deal) with customer complaints but today I'm helping Renée.

40 At the moment, Pete .... (talk) to Davina about the quality control problem.

41 Helena is usually in her office in the afternoon but she .... (work) from home today.

42 Normally delivery .... (take) about three weeks.

SKILLS

A **Match the sentence beginnings with the endings.**

0   I need some training to do ——— a)   costs.

43 It's really important   b)   my job properly.

44 Why don't you buy   c)   a self-study course?

45 We don't have   d)   at home?

46 We have to cut   e)   possible.

47 I'm sorry, it's not   f)   any money for this.

48 How about studying   g)   to me.

B **Complete the conversation with the phrases (a–g).**

a)   I think we need to target younger people

b)   I really like that idea

c)   ~~I agree with you~~

d)   Let's use Facebook and Twitter

e)   How about starting a Facebook page

f)   What about using social networking sites

g)   I don't agree

Tania   I think we need to send out e-mail advertisements.

Franco   I agree with you ⁰. I think that's a great idea. Diana, what do you think?

Diana   I'm afraid .... ⁴⁹.

Franco   Why not?

Diana   .... ⁵⁰. They don't really use e-mail.

Tania   So what should we do?

Diana   .... ⁵¹?

Franco   What, you mean like Facebook and Twitter?

Diana   Yes.

Tania   .... ⁵². In fact, I think it's brilliant.

Franco   .... ⁵³?

Franco   Good idea. But what about Twitter?

Diana   .... ⁵⁴.

C **Complete the sentences with words and phrases from the box.**

| end   ~~presentation~~   sections   subject   subject of   talk about   talk to you |

0   By the end of my *presentation*, you will have a clear idea of our plans.

55 My .... today is our sales strategy.

56 I'd like to .... about our bonus scheme.

57 The .... my presentation is export sales.

58 By the .... of my talk, you will understand why this is necessary.

59 I'm going to .... our manufacturing process.

60 My presentation is in three ....

Answer key

Entry test

Listening (10 marks)
See page 38 for audio script.

1 b **2** c **3** a **4** b **5** c
6 c **7** a **8** b **9** c **10** a

Vocabulary (20 marks)

11 a	**18** c	**25** Japanese
12 h	**19** e	**26** meeting
13 b	**20** month	**27** cake
14 i	**21** company	**28** terrible
15 g	**22** busy	**29** telephone
16 f	**23** expensive	**30** Monday
17 d	**24** car park	

Language (20 marks)

31 you	**38** has	**45** a
32 me	**39** are	**46** c
33 it	**40** is	**47** b
34 your	**41** am	**48** b
35 My	**42** comes	**49** a
36 his	**43** don't	**50** c
37 him	**44** have	

Skills (15 marks)

51 c **52** j **53** i **54** a **55** e **56** b
57 h **58** g **59** f **60** d **61** b **62** a
63 d **64** c **65** e

Reading (15 marks)

66 True
67 False
68 False
69 False
70 True
71 Ilse's
72 late
73 a phone call
74 tomorrow
75 Dimitri
76 22
77 10
78 23
79 24
80 7

Progress test 1

Listening (10 marks)
See page 39 for audio script.

1 b **2** a **3** c **4** a **5** b
6 Sanchez
7 Marketing
8 4922
9 568
10 11.00 a.m.

Vocabulary (20 marks)
11 Poland
12 Polish
13 Friday
14 August
15 Barcelona
16 golf
17 a restaurant
18 c
19 h
20 g
21 a
22 f
23 b
24 e
25 big
26 long
27 relaxing
28 noisy
29 interesting
30 expensive

Language (15 marks)
31 Are
32 What's
33 Where
34 Is
35 What
36 Does
37 works
38 How
39 don't
40 They're usually busy in the afternoon.
41 Why do you need the money?
42 He's never at work before nine o'clock.
43 How much does this cost?
44 Dean sometimes walks to work.
45 How often do you work on Sunday?

Skills *(15 marks)*

46 b **47** a **48** g **49** f **50** c
51 h **52** e **53** d **54** c **55** h
56 a **57** f **58** b **59** e **60** d

Reading *(10 marks)*

61 False
62 True
63 True
64 False
65 True
66 c **67** b **68** b **69** a **70** c

Writing *(10 marks)*

See page 44 for Guidelines for the examiner.
At the weekend, I usually get up at nine o'clock. I often have a big breakfast. Sometimes I play tennis. I often go to the gym. I never have lunch. In the afternoon, I love running. I don't like watching TV. I usually go to a restaurant in the evening. I usually go to bed at eleven o'clock.

Progress test 2

Listening *(10 marks)*

See page 40 for audio script.
1 b **2** a **3** c **4** b **5** b
6 a **7** a **8** c **9** a **10** b

Vocabulary *(18 marks)*

11 book
12 go through
13 watch
14 collect
15 take
16 check in
17 dessert
18 Cabbage
19 tip
20 Sushi
21 'check'
22 Pâté
23 interest-free credit
24 three-year guarantee
25 after-sales service
26 a big discount
27 Free delivery
28 a low deposit

Language *(18 marks)*

29 doesn't
30 Does
31 do
32 don't
33 don't
34 do
35 much
36 many
37 some
38 any
39 any
40 much
41 went
42 was
43 read
44 discussed
45 is
46 gives

Skills *(14 marks)*

47 c
48 a
49 h
50 f
51 b
52 e
53 d
54 close
55 comes
56 weighs
57 's / is
58 costs
59 includes
60 deliver

Reading *(10 marks)*

61 False
62 True
63 False
64 False
65 True
66 b
67 c
68 a
69 b
70 a

Writing *(10 marks)*

See page 44 for Guidelines for the examiner.
To: The Royal Hotel
Subject: Booking
Dear Sir/Madam
I want to book a room at your hotel. I'd like one single room for two nights from 4th to 6th April. I prefer a non-smoking room.
Please can you confirm the price for bed and breakfast?
Also, do you have a car park?
Many thanks.
Best regards,
(Name)

Progress test 3

Listening *(10 marks)*
See page 41 for audio script.

1   b
2   c
3   a
4   Cindy Lee
5   Cindy Lee
6   Cindy Lee
7   Tony Wong
8   Tony Wong
9   Agnes Goh
10   Agnes Goh

Vocabulary *(14 marks)*

11   luxury
12   Niche
13   home
14   Export
15   six thousand, three hundred and seventy
16   twenty-nine thousand, six hundred and six
17   nine hundred and two thousand
18   four million, two hundred and twenty-five thousand and ninety-four
19   twelve point six per cent
20   a
21   d
22   b
23   c
24   e

Language *(18 marks)*

25   Did John leave the company?
26   Why did Lorraine move to Singapore?
27   Ivan wasn't happy at work.
28   Do you have a lot of work?
29   Why was Alfredo stressed?
30   They don't have a lot of time.
31   faster
32   The slowest
33   more efficient
34   less efficient
35   better
36   the best
37   'm/am walking
38   calls
39   don't deal
40   's/is talking
41   's/is working
42   takes

Skills *(18 marks)*

43   g   44   c   45   f   46   a   47   e   48   d   49   g
50   a   51   f   52   b   53   e   54   d
55   subject
56   talk to you
57   subject of
58   end
59   talk about
60   sections

Reading *(10 marks)*

61   False
62   True
63   True
64   False
65   True
66   a   67   c   68   c   69   a   70   b

Writing *(10 marks)*
See page 44 for Guidelines for the examiner.

Dear Tony

I prefer to travel with Britannic. It's more expensive than E-Z Air but the airport is closer to London. The journey time is shorter and the train ticket is cheaper. We can also have a free meal during the flight. There are more flights each day and the flights arrive earlier. With E-Z Air, we arrive at 10.50 p.m. I think that's too late!

All the best
(your name)

Dear Tony

I prefer to travel with E-Z Air. It's much cheaper than Britannic. The cost of getting from the airport to the city centre by train is only a little more. There is no free meal on the flight and it arrives late in the evening but, for me, these are not important. What do you think?

All the best
(your name)

Progress test 4

Listening *(10 marks)*
See page 42 for audio script.

1   a   2   b   3   c   4   b   5   b
6   c   7   c   8   a   9   b   10   a

Vocabulary *(16 marks)*

11   i   12   b   13   f   14   a   15   h   16   g   17   e
18   d   19   a   20   d   21   g   22   b   23   i   24   h
25   c   26   f

Language *(18 marks)*

27   'm/am going to
28   'll
29   will
30   won't

31 'm not going to
32 'll
33 Would
34 Could
35 should
36 shouldn't
37 should
38 Could
39 've visited
40 spent
41 Have you visited
42 went
43 Did you like
44 haven't travelled

Skills *(16 marks)*

45 f   46 i   47 h   48 a   49 b   50 e   51 g
52 d   53 i   54 e   55 a   56 h   57 g   58 b
59 f   60 c

Reading *(10 marks)*

61 False
62 True
63 False
64 False
65 True
66 b   67 a   68 c   69 c   70 b

Writing *(10 marks)*

See page 44 for Guidelines for the examiner.

Dear Sergei

Yes, I remember you. I would like to see you again. I'm afraid I'm very busy next week and I can't make Wednesday. How about lunch on Tuesday or Thursday? I'm free between one and two o'clock on those days. There's a nice restaurant near my office. Could you bring a sample of your company's products?

Best wishes,

(your name)

Exit test

Listening *(10 marks)*

See page 43 for audio script.

1 7 p.m.
2 factory
3 sales team
4 out to dinner
5 samples
6 contracts
7 launch
8 advertising
9 11 a.m.
10 flight details

Vocabulary *(14 marks)*

11 in
12 a niche
13 employs
14 face-to-face

15 too far
16 punctual
17 deposit
18 booking
19 a workforce
20 annual leave
21 an order
22 stock
23 the receipt
24 a tip

Language *(18 marks)*

25 b   26 c   27 c   28 a   29 b   30 c
31 landed
32 are you doing
33 's/is
34 've/have had
35 'm/am waiting
36 'll/will call
37 can't
38 Are
39 aren't
40 a little
41 should
42 don't

Skills *(18 marks)*

43 f   44 j   45 a   46 i   47 b   48 h
49 e   50 g   51 d   52 j   53 d   54 a
55 i   56 h   57 b   58 g   59 c   60 f

Reading *(10 marks)*

61 False   62 True   63 False   64 False
65 True   66 False   67 True   68 False
69 True   70 False

Writing *(10 marks)*

See page 44 for Guidelines for the examiner.

Subject: Visit from the Spanish sales office

Dear team

In our meeting earlier today, we discussed the programme for the visit and agreed the following. Simon is going to arrange a taxi from the hotel to the factory for 9.00 a.m. arrival. The sales team will join us for coffee and an informal talk at 9.30. Eleanor will lead the meeting at 10.15. We're having lunch in the company restaurant at 1.00 and, in the afternoon, Frederick will take the visitors on a tour of the factory. We'll have question-and-answer time and coffee led by Corinne at 4.15 and after that, at 6.00, the Spanish team will return to their hotel. Eduardo is going to organise the evening activities.

If you have any questions, let me know.

Best regards,

(your name)

READING **A** Read the article and decide if the statements are true or false.

0 People rarely chat about products or services on Facebook. *False*

61 The article says that Facebook is good at reaching small markets.

62 Facebook's user data is very useful for advertisers.

63 Starbucks uses Facebook to learn about its customers.

64 Companies have to spend a lot of money to advertise on Facebook.

65 Facebook earns most of its money from advertising.

Social advertising:
Lower costs and a personal relationship

People use Facebook to complain about or praise companies and products, from airlines to biscuits. That's why social media marketing is important for advertisers. Facebook can help advertisers reach hundreds of millions of possible customers – a huge market.

Facebook has a lot of information about its users, including people's interests and their friends. Advertisers can use this information. It helps them get the right message to the right person at the right time.

Starbucks, the coffee retailer, created its first page a few years ago. The page helped the company understand the things people liked – and disliked. It then used that information to help create its more traditional advertising campaigns. It also used the advertising campaigns to draw more people to its Facebook pages, which have tens of millions of fans.

It's an inexpensive way to attract new customers and it allows the company to build a close relationship with them.

Every time Facebook showed the ad to 1,000 people or every time a person clicked on one of the ads, Starbucks paid Facebook. Ads usually cost less than $1 per click. More than 90 per cent of Facebook revenues come from advertising, according to EMarketer, a research firm.

B Read the article again. Then choose the best option – a, b or c – to complete the sentences.

0 Facebook is a natural way to advertise, because people often use it to
  talk about products or services .

   a) contact companies

   b) meet new friends

   (c)) talk about products or services.

66 Advertisers like Facebook because it helps them to ....

   a) reach a big market

   b) deal with cultural problems

   c) sell products cheaply

67 Facebook helps companies understand their ....

   a) products

   b) employees

   c) market

68 After setting up a Facebook page, Starbucks ....

    a) had a huge increase in sales.

    b) stopped most of its traditional advertising

    c) used the information to improve its traditional advertisements

69 Facebook helps businesses to build relationships with ....

    a) customers

    b) other businesses

    c) advertising agencies

70 Starbucks paid Facebook for an advertisement ....

    a) but they didn't know how many people saw it.

    b) when people viewed or clicked on it.

    c) before the ad appeared on the internet.

WRITING

You and your colleague Tony need to fly to London for a meeting. You can choose between two airlines. Write an e-mail to Tony comparing the two airlines. Say which one you prefer to travel with and why. Write 60–70 words.

	Britannic	**E-Z Air**
Cost	€350	€180
Fly to	Heathrow Airport – close to London – train to city centre takes about 15 minutes and costs about €22.	Stansted Airport – about 55 km from London – train takes about 45 minutes and costs about €26.
Free meal during flight?	Yes	No
Flights each day	3	1
Arrival times	9.55 a.m. 3.45 p.m. 7.00 p.m.	10.50 p.m.

Progress test 4 (Units 10–12)

🔊 **7 British worker Alison Crabbe spent six months working in Seoul in the South Korea office of her company. Her colleague James Ronson asks her about her time in Korea. Choose the best word or phrase – a, b or c – to complete the sentences.**

0   Alison says that her work in the Seoul office was . ꞓ𝘯𝘵𝘦𝘳𝘦𝘴𝘵𝘪𝘯𝘨 . .

   (**a**) interesting   **b**) hard   **c**) a little boring

1   In the Seoul office, clothes are .... in Britain.

   a) more formal than

   b) less formal than

   c) about the same as

2   Most of the women in the office wore ....

   a) a business suit   **b**) a uniform   **c**) glasses

3   The atmosphere in the office seemed very ....

   a) serious   **b**) relaxed   **c**) professional

4   The working day began at ....

   a) 8.15   **b**) 8.30   **c**) 8.45

5   At the start of the working day, everyone talks to their ....

   a) co-workers   **b**) manager   **c**) customers

6   .... late.

   a) A lot of people arrive

   b) A few people arrive

   c) No one arrives

7   At 5.15, the workers ....

   a) take a break   **b**) go home   **c**) continue working

8   The workers don't want to leave the office before ....

   a) the boss   **b**) Alison   **c**) the cleaner

9   After work, people sometimes go to ....

   a) the boss's house   **b**) a restaurant   **c**) a meeting

10 Alison didn't like the ....

   a) meetings   **b**) long hours   **c**) food

VOCABULARY   **A**   **Match the sentences with the same meaning.**

0   At the end of the week, we have a meeting where people discuss subjects.

11 We have a lot of meetings where information or instructions are given.

12 We often move documents from the network to a PC.

13 We think it's important to have direct contact with other people.

14 We often move documents from a PC to the network.

15 We don't have to wear business suits at the end of the week.

16 Our meetings are informal.

17 We can work from nine to five or from ten to six.

18 Every year, we have three weeks' holiday.

a) We upload a lot of work to the intranet.

b) We download a lot of work from the intranet.

c) We have a forum on Fridays.

d) We have a system of annual leave.

e) We have a flexitime system.

f) We value face-to-face meetings.

g) We have relaxed meetings.

h) We have casual Fridays.

i) We often have briefings.

B   **Match the underlined words in the text with the definitions.**

> We are a customer-focused[0] company that supports innovation[19]. We need an experienced manager to set up[20] a new branch in a challenging overseas market. We currently have limited sales in the market. Your main objective will be to increase[21] sales. You will need to improve[22] communication with our local distributor. You will need to lead[23] a team, train[24] new staff and develop[25] new products for the market. We will reward[26] good performance.

a) welcomes new ideas and change ☐

b) make better ☐

c) create ☐

d) start ☐

e) putting needs and wants of customers first ☐ 0

f) offer incentives for ☐

g) make more ☐

h) teach ☐

i) be in charge of ☐

LANGUAGE   **A**   **Complete the conversations with the correct form of *will* or *going to*.**

Conversation 1

A   My company is going out of business. They sent everyone home today.

B   Oh, no. What . *are you going to* .⁰ do?

A   I ....²⁷ start my own company.

Conversation 2

A   I have to move these boxes.

B   I ....²⁸ help you.

A   Really? Thanks!

Conversation 3

A   Computer keyboards ....²⁹ disappear in the next ten years. Everything will be voice activated.

B   You're right. We ....³⁰ need keyboards in the future.

Conversation 4

A   Have you made your schedule for next week?

B   Yes. I ....³¹ have any meetings with clients.

A   Oh, good.

Conversation 5

A   Goodbye!

B   Goodbye! I ....³² see you next week!

B   **Choose the best words to complete the conversation.**

A   Look at the time.

B   It's six o'clock. We ((should)/ would)⁰ go. We don't want to be late.

A   (Could / Would)³³ you like to walk to the restaurant? It isn't far.

B   That's a good idea.

A   (Should / Could)³⁴ you bring a copy of the report, please? We may want to discuss it.

B   I don't think we (should / would)³⁵ take that.

A   Why not?

B   We (shouldn't / wouldn't)³⁶ directly discuss business at this meal. They don't do business that way here.

A   But it's a business dinner.

B   Yes, but we (would / should)³⁷ get to know each other, too. That's very important here.

A   (Could / Should)³⁸ you explain something to me?

B   Sure.

A   How are we going to make a deal if we don't talk about business?

B   You need to be patient!

C **Complete the conversation with the correct form (past simple or present perfect) of the verbs in brackets.**

A   Do you travel a lot for work?

B   Yes. Since I started the job two years ago, I 've travelled.⁰ (travel) abroad more

than thirty times and I ....³⁹ (visit) more than ten different countries.

Last month, I ....⁴⁰ (spend) two weeks in Bahrain and Kuwait.

A   Wow. That's interesting......................⁴¹ (you visit) the United Arab Emirates?

B   Yes. I ....⁴² (go) there last year.

A   ....⁴³ (you like) it?

B   Yes, it was fantastic.

A   I ....⁴⁴ (not travel) anywhere yet this year but next month I'm going to

Spain on holiday.

SKILLS **A** **Match the sentences with the responses.**

0   What time is good for you?

45   What's a good day for you?

46   We could meet the other members of the team.

47   There's something I'd like to talk to you about.

48   Do you have any special strengths?

49   What do you do in your free time?

50   What did you learn from your last job?

51   I think we should stop meeting Dave every week.

52   I can make 15th January.

a)   People say I'm good at giving presentations.

b)   I spend a lot of time reading.

c)   How about 4.15?

d)   I'm afraid I can't make that date.

e)   I improved my organisational skills.

f)   27th March would be fine.

g)   Mmm. I don't think that's a good idea. He's important to us.

h)   OK. Would you like to go in my office?

i)   I agree. Let's meet them next week.

B **Complete the conversations with the phrases (a–i).**

a) There's a problem with

b) My main aim is to become

c) I had a problem with

d) ~~I'm sorry I~~

e) The traffic was

f) My main skills are

g) Let's talk to

h) We should move him to

i) My flight was

Conversation 1

A *I'm sorry I* [0] missed our meeting on Tuesday. ....[53] late.

B Don't worry. Ajay missed it, too. We changed the meeting to tomorrow.

Conversation 2

A What happened?

B ....[54] very bad. There's a lot of snow and ice on the roads.

Conversation 3

A We need to talk about the staff in this department. ....[55] Andreas.

B I know. ....[56] another department.

A I agree. ....[57] him.

Conversation 4

A What do you want to do in the future?

B ....[58] a manager.

Conversation 5

A What are you good at?

B ....[59] advertising and marketing.

Conversation 6

A What didn't you like about your last job?

B Well, ...[60] working too much overtime.

READING **A** **Read the article and decide if the statements are true or false.**

0 E-mail messages ALL IN CAPITAL LETTERS seem rude. *True*

61 It isn't important to write polite e-mails.

62 Speaking directly to people is sometimes very useful.

63 Nowadays, it's OK to keep your phone switched on all the time.

64 The rules are the same for e-mail and online chat rooms.

65 Sometimes, abbreviations like *GR8* are fine.

How to use e-mail (politely)

A New Zealand healthcare company fired Vicki Walker because she wrote her e-mail messages IN CAPITAL LETTERS. Politeness experts say that using all capitals in an e-mail is like shouting. However, it can be difficult to know the 'rules' of politeness in writing e-mails. Here are some expert opinions:

Emily Post Institute, a US company that gives training in manners and politeness:

- Don't communicate only electronically. Face-to-face communication is also very important.

- Avoid typing your message in capital letters. Also be careful to avoid angry words.

- Think of your electronic communication as a conversation.

Debrett's, a UK company that provides manners and politeness training:

- People are more important than gadgets. If possible, turn off your phone in social situations.

- Don't put your phone on the dining table or look at it a lot during conversations.

Matthew Strawbridge, an expert on Internet politeness:

- Use normal capitalisation and punctuation in e-mail messages. In online chat rooms, you can use entirely or mainly lower case letters if you like.

- In chat rooms, you may use abbreviations (e.g. GR8 = great) but you should explain them if the other person doesn't understand.

B **Choose the best word or phrases – a, b or c – to complete the sentences.**

0 Vicki Walker's company thought her e-mails were .... *rude* ....
   (a) rude   **b)** not clear   **c)** full of mistakes

66 Typing everything in capitals isn't polite, because it's like ....
   a) a road sign   **b)** talking loudly   **c)** a child's writing

67 It's best .... e-mails with angry words when you feel angry or upset.
   a) not to write   **b)** to send   **c)** not to read

68 .... can be like talking.
   a) Reading a letter
   b) Meetings
   c) E-mails and text messages

69 In online chat rooms, it's normal to use .... letters.
   a) no lower case   **b)** mostly capital   **c)** all lower case

70 Sometimes when you are in an online chat room, you must ....
   abbreviations.
   a) use   **b)** explain   **c)** feel angry about

WRITING You receive this e-mail. Write a reply. Say that you are very busy next week but you would like to meet Sergei again. Suggest lunch at a nice restaurant near your office. You are free on Tuesday or Thursday between 1 p.m. and 2 p.m. Ask him to bring a sample of his company's products, if possible. Write 50–60 words.

From:	Sergei Kozlov

Hello.

We met at a conference in Stuttgart last September. I'm going to be in your area next week. Could we meet for dinner on Wednesday evening? Please let me know if you have time and which day you would prefer.

Hope to see you soon.

Best wishes,

Sergei Kozlov

Exit test (General review)

🔊 8 Listen to the telephone conversation. Robert is planning to make a business trip to see David. Complete David's notes.

Robert's visit next ....month....[0]

Mon 16 Apr
— arriving at ....[1]

Tue 17 Apr
— visit the ....[2] in the morning
— meet the ....[3] in the afternoon
— go ....[4] in the evening — Robert will bring some
  ....[5] to show

Wed 18 Apr
— Eugene wants to discuss ....[6]
— Robert wants to talk with Eugene about next year's ....[7] and the
  plans for ....[8]

Thur 19 Apr
— Flight at ....[9]

Next action: Robert will e-mail ....[10]

VOCABULARY

A **Choose the best words to complete the text.**

Karina is (Mexico /(Mexican))[0] but she lives and works in London. She started her job last year, (in / at)[11] April. She loves her work. She sells special-interest holidays. It's (an export / a niche)[12] market and she really enjoys the work of planning specialised tours for clients. The company is very small. It (employs / supplies)[13] only four people and they all work in one office. This makes (print / face-to-face)[14] communication very easy. They can talk to each other at any time.

Next week, she's moving to a new flat because her old one is (too far / far enough)[15] from the office. She's a very (punctual / practical)[16] person – she likes to be on time – and the long journey to work was difficult. She had a lot of problems with train and bus delays. She's also buying some new furniture for the flat. She doesn't have a lot of money so she paid a (deposit / deal)[17] of ten per cent and she'll make monthly payments. The furniture will be delivered next week.

B **Complete the conversations with words and phrases from the box.**

> ~~a sales conference~~   a tip   a workforce   an order   annual leave   booking
> stock   the receipt

Conversation 1

A   Kevin has organised .$\underset{}{a\ sales\ conference}$.^{0} for 25th–26th July.

B   I know. And I'm planning to return from my holiday on 27th July!

A   Oh, no. Can you change your holiday .... ^{18}?

B   I'm not sure.

Conversation 2

A   How big is your company?

B   Big! It has .... ^{19} of about 18,000 people.

A   How much .... ^{20} do you get each year?

B   Three weeks.

Conversation 3

A   I'd like to place .... ^{21} for 100 boxes of item 20091. Are the goods in .... ^{22}?

B   Yes, they are.

Conversation 4

A   Do you have .... ^{23} from dinner last night? I need it for my expense records.

B   Yes, here it is.

A   Did you leave .... ^{24} for the waiter?

B   No, I didn't. I thought you did!

LANGUAGE

A **Choose the best word or phrase – a, b or c – to complete the sentences.**

0   Dirk .....$\underset{}{isn't}$..... Italian.

    a) isn't   **b)** aren't   **c)** am not

25   A   .... are you from?

    B   Japan.

    a) What   **b)** Where   **c)** Who

26   .... Ricardo drive to work?

    a) Is   **b)** Do   **c)** Does

27   Oscar .... from home.

    a) sometime work   **b)** works sometimes   **c)** sometimes works

28   Mr Albert .... to meetings.

    a) doesn't go   **b)** not go   **c)** isn't go

29   This office building .... a meeting room.

    a) not have   **b)** doesn't have   **c)** hasn't

30   A   Can Yusuf speak German?

    B   Yes, ...

    a) can he   **b)** can   **c)** he can

B **Complete the extract of a phone conversation with the correct form of the verbs in brackets.**

A   When _did you arrive_[0] (you arrive) in Thailand?

B   Yesterday. My flight ....[31] (land) at about three o'clock in the afternoon.

A   And what ....[32] (you do) now?

B   Well, it ....[33] (be) nine in the morning here now. I ....[34] (have) my breakfast and now I ....[35] (wait) for a taxi. In fact, the taxi is here now! I ....[36] (call) you later, OK?

C **Complete the conversations with words and phrases from the box.**

| a little   are   aren't   ~~can~~   can't   don't   should |

Conversation 1

A   .... _Can_ ....[0] you speak Japanese?

B   No, I ....[37].

Conversation 2

A   ....[38] there any visitors in the office today?

B   No, there ....[39].

Conversation 3

A   How much is the RX-100?

B   It's ....[40] more expensive than the RX-90.

Conversation 4

A   Do you think we ....[41] talk to Ramon?

B   No, I ....[42].

SKILLS **A** **Match the sentences with the responses.**

0   How about a cup of tea?   a)   Yes, there is.

43   Do you like football?   b)   OK, I'll take a look at one.

44   Can I speak to Jorge Ramos, please?   c)   Yes, please.

45   Is there a car park?   d)   I learned how to be patient.

46   My suggestion is to go for a cocktail.   e)   OK. What is it?

47   Why don't you buy a self-study course?   f)   Yes, I do.

48   What do you think?   g)   How about Wednesday?

49   There's something I'd like to talk to you about.   h)   I think we need to target young people.

        i)   That's a great idea.

50   What day suits you?   j)   I'm afraid he isn't in the office today.

51   What did you learn from your last job?

B Complete the conversations with the phrases (a–j).

a) What's

b) My subject today is

c) One thing we could do is

d) I think

e) ~~I have a problem with~~

f) I really enjoy

g) I'm afraid I can't make

h) What about using

i) I need some

j) Can I have your

0 A ~~*I have a problem with*~~ my new camera.

   B Oh dear. I'm sorry to hear that.

52 A .... credit card details, please?

   B It's a MasterCard. The number is ...

53 A .... Pascal's is the best restaurant. The food is delicious.

   B Yes, I agree. The food is great.

54 A .... the target market?

   B It's aimed at stylish young men who want to look good.

55 A .... training to do my job properly.

   B I'm sorry. It's just not possible.

56 A .... social networking sites?

   B I'm not sure that's a good idea.

57 A What are you going to talk about?

   B .... our new product line.

58 A Is 25th May OK for you?

   B .... 25th May.

59 A There's a problem with Astrid.

   B I agree. .... talk to her.

60 A What do you do in your free time?

   B .... sports.

Read the article and decide if the statements are true or false.

0   Management styles haven't changed much in the past fifty years.   *False*

61   The biggest problem for 21st-century managers is controlling employees.

62   In the 21st century, power comes from doing good work.

63   Microsoft is a good example of 20th-century management style.

64   At Microsoft, managers watch workers' hours very carefully.

65   It's important for managers to get to know different types of people.

66   Making decisions is one of the main jobs of a 21st-century manager.

67   Good managers understand their teams' thoughts and feelings.

68   Global managers should try to ignore cultural issues as much as possible.

69   For Gary Kildare, respect is more important than speaking a lot of languages.

70   Face-to-face communication is the most important part of 21st-century management.

Turning bosses into cross-cultural coaches

In the 20th century, managers often worked to control employees. But 21st-century management has different rules. Twenty-first century managers should prepare to be coaches rather than bosses. They should influence and work with their team rather than control it.

Some experts believe that, in the 21st century, people will have power in the workplace because of what they do, not because they have the word 'manager' in their job title.

The Microsoft office near Amsterdam is a good example of this style of work. Managers here don't control workers, they trust them. Managers don't count the hours that workers spend in the office, they look at the work that employees produce.

Management experts recommend that managers should spend time with colleagues from different backgrounds. The manager of the future will be a coach who helps the team succeed, not the person who makes all the decisions. Coaching a team requires an understanding of the motivations and experience of the people in the team.

Cultural sensitivity is very important in managing global teams, says Gary Kildare, a vice-president of human resources at IBM, the technology group. 'You can't speak 20 languages but you can respect everyone's culture. In some cultures people are quiet, in others they are not,' he says. 'It is about treating and respecting everyone as an individual.'

Regular communication is essential. 'It can take longer to build trusting relationships because you don't always have that face-to-face contact with people.'

WRITING

You had a meeting with your colleagues to make plans for visitors from the Spanish sales office. Use the programme and notes to write an informal e-mail report of the meeting. Write 100–120 words.

Time	Programme	Notes
9.00 a.m.	Spanish team arrives at factory	*Who's going to arrange their taxi from the hotel? – Simon*
9.30 a.m.	Coffee and informal talk	*Who should come? – the sales team*
10.15 a.m.	Meeting	*Who should lead the meeting? – Eleanor*
1.00 p.m.	Lunch	*Company restaurant or local Chinese restaurant? – Company restaurant*
Afternoon	Factory tour	*Who will lead tour? – Frederick*
4.15 p.m.	Question-and-answer time and coffee	*Who will lead this? – Corinne*
6.00 p.m.	Spanish team return to hotel before evening activities	*Who will organise the evening activities? – Eduardo*

Subject: Visit from the Spanish sales office

Dear team

In our meeting earlier today, we discussed the programme for the visit and agreed the following. Simon ...

Audio scripts

The recordings of the material below can be found on the *Test Master CD-ROM*, which is at the back of the *Teacher's Resource Book*. Play each recording twice.

Entry test

🔊 1

Conversation 1
A   Roberto!
B   Oh, hi, Lars!
A   Roberto, what time is our conference call with Tokyo this morning?
B   It starts in fifteen minutes – at ten o'clock.
A   Ten o'clock? OK, thanks.

Conversation 2
A   Are you ready to order?
B   Yes. I'd like the grilled fish, please.
A   Grilled fish. OK. And for you, sir?
C   I'll have the roast duck.
A   The roast duck. All right. Can I bring you anything else? Bread? Olives?
B   Some bread, yes.
C   And some olives, please.

Conversation 3
A   Excuse me. Is the train station near here?
B   It's not far. Go straight along this street and past the post office. Take the first left.
A   First left. OK.
B   And you'll see the train station on your right, just across the road from the big hotel.
A   Is it nearby? My train leaves in 15 minutes.
B   No problem. You can walk there in two minutes.
A   OK. Thanks very much!

Conversation 4
A   Can I help you?
B   Yes. My name's Roberts – James Roberts. I have a reservation.
A   Hello, Mr Roberts. Let's see … yes … it's a single room, smoking, for three nights.
B   It's a single room but I asked for non-smoking. I don't smoke.
A   I'm sorry about that. So it's a single, non-smoking room for three nights?
B   Yes, that's right.
A   OK. We'll put you in room 332. It's on the third floor.

Conversation 5
A   Excuse me.
B   Yes?
A   Do you have any German newspapers?
B   Let's see … . I have *Bild*. It's €2.50.
A   I'll take it. Er … how much is it?
B   Two euros and fifty cents.
A   Here you go.
B   Thanks.

Progress test 1

🔊 2–3

Alan	Technical Support, Alan speaking. How can I help?
Sofia	Hello. This is Sofia Sanchez from Marketing. I have a problem with my computer.
Alan	What's the problem?
Sofia	It's my e-mail. It doesn't work. I can't read or send e-mails.
Alan	Hmm. Are you connected to the Internet?
Sofia	Er ... I don't know.
Alan	Can you use the web?
Sofia	Uh ... no, I can't. I can't see any web pages.
Alan	OK, so you have a problem with the Internet connection. We'll send a technician to look at it. Let me take your details. It's Sofia ...
Sofia	Sofia Sanchez. S-A-N-C-H-E-Z.
Alan	And your department?
Sofia	Marketing.
Alan	Right. And what's your phone number?
Sofia	It's 4922.
Alan	4922? OK. And the problem is with your computer's e-mail and Internet connection.
Sofia	That's right.
Alan	And what's your office number?
Sofia	I'm in office number 568.
Alan	568. OK, I'll send a technician.
Sofia	Can he come this morning? I have a meeting this afternoon and I have a lot of work!
Alan	What time is your meeting?
Sofia	It's at two o'clock.
Alan	Two o'clock? OK ... let me see. How about eleven o'clock?
Sofia	OK. Yes, eleven o'clock is good.

Progress test 2

🔊 4

Receptionist	Hello, Mayfield Electrical Products. How can I help you?
Pablo	Hello. Can I speak to Andrea Thomas, please?
Receptionist	Just a moment. I'll put you through.
Andrea	Andrea Thomas speaking.
Pablo	Hi, Andrea. This is Pablo Martinez.
Andrea	Hello, Mr Martinez. What can I do for you?
Pablo	I'm calling about the BZ-149s we spoke about yesterday.
Andrea	OK.
Pablo	Before I place an order, I have some questions.
Andrea	Sure. Go ahead.
Pablo	Well, firstly, do you give a guarantee?
Andrea	Yes. It's two years on all our models.
Pablo	Two years?
Andrea	That's right. But customers very rarely have problems.
Pablo	OK. And what about a deposit?
Andrea	Well, we ask for a 15-per-cent-deposit on large orders – that's more than 100 units.
Pablo	And what's the deposit on an order below 100 units?
Andrea	For small orders, we ask for full payment – 100 per cent – in advance.
Pablo	Oh, OK. And do you have the goods in stock?
Andrea	That depends on the size of your order. Right now, we have about 110 BZ-149s in stock. How many do you need?
Pablo	We only need 50.
Andrea	So you're fine.
Pablo	OK, I think that's everything. I need to check a couple of other details here in my office but I'll contact you again this afternoon.
Andrea	Great. You can call me on my mobile. Do you have that number?
Pablo	Is it 08891-988-033?
Andrea	That's right.
Pablo	OK. I'll talk to you later.
Andrea	OK. Goodbye.

Progress test 3

 5–6

Marco	OK, the next thing we need to talk about is the new leader for the South China team. I think we need to choose someone from the Hong Kong office. The three choices are Cindy Lee, Tony Wong or Agnes Goh. Susan, what do you think?
Susan	I prefer Cindy Lee. She's reliable and very hard-working.
Marco	How do you feel about that, Elaine?
Elaine	Well, I don't know. She's a great salesperson because she's ambitious but she doesn't listen. She doesn't work well with a team. I prefer Tony Wong. He's creative and really sociable.
Susan	Sorry, I don't agree with you. He's too relaxed. He makes an excellent team member but not a good team leader.
Marco	OK. So what about Agnes Goh? She's practical …
Elaine	… but not motivating. She's just not a natural leader.
Marco	I'm not sure I agree with you. What about talking to the team? We can see what they think.
Susan	Great idea, Marco.

Progress test 4

🔊 7

James	So, how did you like working in the Seoul office?
Alison	It was good. It was really interesting – very different from working here.
James	What do you mean?
Alison	Well, first of all, the atmosphere was very formal. Everyone wore formal clothes. In fact, most of the women wore a uniform.
James	Really?
Alison	Yes. And the men all wore suits. I liked that. It felt very professional. If you look good, you feel good!
James	Hmm. What else?
Alison	The start of the working day was also very formal. Work starts at eight thirty, and everyone is there on time, ready to work. A bit of music plays and the working day begins. And then everyone tells their manager their plan for the day.
James	Really? So nobody arrives late?
Alison	Well, no, not really.
James	Amazing. What about at the end of the day?
Alison	Well, again, a bit of music plays to signal the end of the working day. It's at quarter past five.
James	Does everyone go home then?
Alison	No, everyone keeps working. They work a lot of overtime in Korea. Most people try to stay in the office until the boss leaves.
James	So they work hard.
Alison	Yes, they do but they have fun, too. After work, we went out to some great restaurants.
James	So, was there anything you didn't like?
Alison	Well, they have a lot of meetings and the meetings take a long time and they can be a bit boring.

Exit test

🔊 8

David	David White.
Robert	Hi, David. It's Robert Haynes here.
David	Hello, Robert. How are you?
Robert	Fine, thanks. I'm calling about my visit next month. Can we talk about the schedule?
David	Yes, sure.
Robert	Well, I'd like to arrive on Monday the 16th of April. Is that OK?
David	Monday the 16th? Yes, that's fine. What time will you arrive?
Robert	There's a flight that arrives at 7 p.m.
David	OK, that's good. I could meet you at the airport and take you to your hotel. Then we could visit the factory on Tuesday morning.
Robert	Great. What about Tuesday afternoon?
David	We could meet the sales team. We have some new salespeople. I think you should meet them.
Robert	That sounds good. Could we meet in the afternoon and then go out to dinner together?
David	Good idea. And could you bring some samples of the new line to show them? They're really excited about it.
Robert	No problem.
David	OK. Then on Wednesday, we can meet with Eugene. He wants to talk about some contracts with you.
Robert	Good. I need to talk with him about next year's launch, too. We need to discuss our plans for advertising.
David	Right, OK.
Robert	I'd like to return home on Thursday morning. There's a flight at eleven. Will that be OK?
David	No problem. So what's next?
Robert	I'll send you an e-mail with my flight details.

Guidelines for the examiner

Writing tests

For each writing task award 10 marks, as follows.

- Including all the information required: 3 marks
- Accuracy of language (grammar and vocabulary): 3 marks
- In the description in Progress test 1: award 3 marks for overall clarity

  In e-mails: award 3 marks for politeness (opening and closing phrases and thanking, where appropriate)
- Organisation and clear structuring of ideas: 1 mark

Model answers to each writing task are given in the Answer key on pages i–iv.